MONSTER KNOWS SHAPES

BY LORI CAPOTE   ILLUSTRATED BY CHIP WASS

PICTURE WINDOW BOOKS
a capstone imprint

Mom wore her spotted sun hat.

We brought some rotten grapes.

We're at the beach today to learn about fun shapes!

A **SQUARE** is one shape you'll find.
The sides are all the same,
like my **RAISIN-STINKBUG SANDWICH**
or my **CATCH-A-CACTUS GAME.**

I think I see a SQUARE right there—
all covered in green slimy vine.

DANGER

Danger—sharks are just offshore.
Read the **SQUARE** wood sign!

6

This beach ball is a **CIRCLE** shape.

We see through **CIRCLES** too.

I like the **CIRCLE JELLYFISH**

that are made of squishy goo!

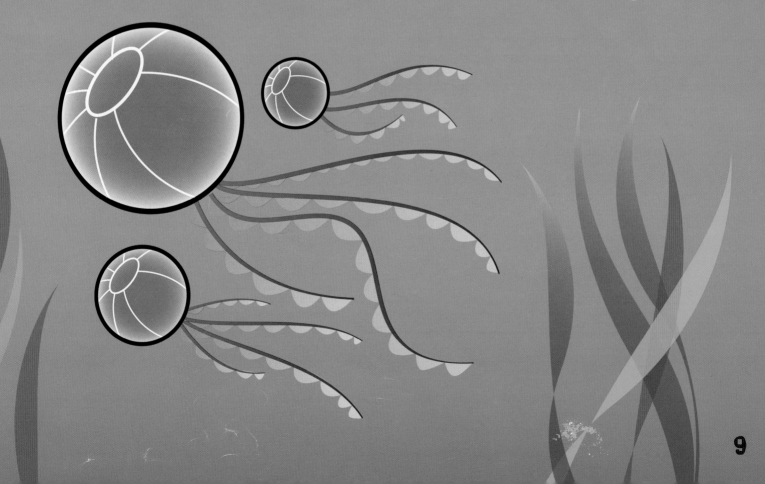

An **OVAL** can be speckled like this snowy plover egg.

And here's an oval **SPIDER**,
if you just ignore its legs!

11

A **TRIANGLE** has three straight sides.
And three points—**1, 2, 3.**
My sailboat has a **TRIANGLE**
to sail across the sea.

I love my muddy sailboat and more **TRIANGLES** too!

My evil castle's topped with them:
RED AND GOLD AND BLUE!

A **STAR** shape has five pointy tips.
A **STARFISH** spreads out wide!

I love this **STAR-SHAPED FLOWER**
that traps a bug inside!

A **RECTANGLE** has four straight sides:
TWO SHORT and then **TWO LONG**.

Check out my **FLOATY RAFT** or all the **BOOKS** I brought along.

I spent one dollar RECTANGLE
on frozen green bean ice.

My towel is a **RECTANGLE**
with holes that feel quite nice.

All of these **SHAPES** are easy to see!

You'll spot them near and far.

Look for shapes while here and there.
Find shapes wherever you are!

Internet Sites

FactHound offers a safe, fun way to find Internet sites related to this book. All of the sites on FactHound have been researched by our staff.

Here's all you do:

Visit *www.facthound.com*

Type in this code: 9781404879485

Super-cool stuff! Check out projects, games and lots more at **www.capstonekids.com**

Look for all the books in the series:

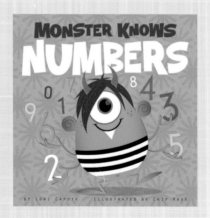

Thanks to our adviser for his expertise, research, and advice:
Terry Flaherty, PhD, Professor of English
Minnesota State University, Mankato

Editor: Shelly Lyons
Designer: Ashlee Suker
Art Director: Nathan Gassman
Production Specialist: Laura Manthe
The illustrations in this book were created digitally.

Picture Window Books are published by Capstone,
1710 Roe Crest Drive, North Mankato, Minnesota 56003
www.capstonepub.com

Library of Congress Cataloging-in-Publication Data
Capote, Lori, 1966-
Monster knows shapes / by Lori Capote ; illustrated by Chip Wass.
pages cm. — (Monster knows math)
ISBN 978-1-4048-7948-5 (library binding)
ISBN 978-1-4048-8041-2 (board book)
ISBN 978-1-4795-0185-4 (eBook PDF)
1. Shapes—Juvenile literature. I. Wass, Chip, 1965- illustrator.
II. Title.
QA445.5.C365 2013
516'.15—dc23   2012029719

Artistic Effects
Shutterstock, background texture (throughout)

Printed in the United States of America in
North Mankato, Minnesota.
092012   006933CGS13